SIMPLY ADVENT

TRACY KRAUSS

Simply Advent

ISBN: 978-1-990871-184 (book); 978-1-990871-191 (pbk)

Published by **Fictitious Ink Publishing**, Tumbler Ridge, BC, Canada, V0C 2W0

INTRODUCTION

Advent is a special season for many Christians around the world and marks a time of anticipation leading up to the celebration of our Saviour's birth. Traditions and variations abound when it comes to celebrating this momentous occasion. This little booklet is not meant to be an exhaustive treatise on the subject. Rather, it is a very simple introduction meant to encourage participants to incorporate Advent into their other seasonal celebrations.

Typically, Advent is marked on the four Sundays before Christmas. A wreath with five candles is most often used. One candle is lit each week culminating in lighting the final large candle in the middle of the wreath on Christmas Eve.

Each Sunday represents something different, although traditions vary from denomination to denomination. As well, some traditions utilize different coloured candles, but this book does not go into those specifics.

Use this little book as a jumping off place to delve further into this rich tradition. God bless you as you celebrate!

THE FIRST SUNDAY OF ADVENT

The first candle of Advent is sometimes called the "Prophets' Candle" and symbolizes "Hope". There are thousands of prophecies relating to Jesus in the Old Testament. It is not the purpose of this book to expound on all of them, but it is exciting to know that we have assurance that Jesus is who He said He was—the Saviour of the World! These prophecies gave great hope to those looking forward to their Messiah and they also give us hope that He will return again, as He said He would.

<u>Scripture:</u>

Matthew 1: 18–25

Now the birth of Jesus Christ took place in this way. When his mother Mary had been betrothed to Joseph, before they came together she was found to be with child from the Holy Spirit. And her husband Joseph, being a just man and unwilling to put her to shame, resolved to divorce her quietly.

But as he considered these things, behold, an angel of the Lord appeared to him in a dream, saying, "Joseph, son of David, do not fear to take Mary as your wife, for that which is conceived in her is from the Holy Spirit. She will bear a son, and you shall call His name Jesus, for He will save his people from their sins." All this took place to fulfill what the Lord had spoken by the prophet:

"Behold, the virgin shall conceive and bear a son, and they shall call his name Immanuel" (which means, God with us). When Joseph woke from sleep, he did as the angel of the Lord commanded him: he took his wife, but knew her not until she had given birth to a son. And he called his name Jesus. (ESV)

Isaiah 7:14

Therefore the Lord Himself will give you a sign. Behold, the virgin shall conceive and bear a son, and shall call His name Immanuel. (ESV)

Prayer focus:

Thank You for the assurance we have from Your Word. You came to this earth as a tiny baby, just the way You said You would. You are Immanuel—our Saviour and Redeemer. As I prepare to celebrate the "reason for the season" help me to keep my eyes fixed on the hope of Your second coming.

You may wish to sing a Christmas carol which focuses on the prophetic aspects of Christ's birth such as 'O Come O Come Emmanuel'.

THE SECOND SUNDAY OF ADVENT

The second candle on the Advent wreath is often referred to as the "Bethlehem Candle" symbolizing "Faith". Isn't it interesting that God chose to enter this world in His human form in such a humble way? He could have chosen to be born in a palace, but instead, He was born in a lowly manger, thus making Himself available to every class of person, no matter their position or pedigree. What God foretold through the prophet Micah came to pass, and Jesus was born in Bethlehem to be our Saviour, Redeemer, and Lord.

<u>Scripture:</u>

Luke 2: 1–7

In those days a decree went out from Caesar Augustus that all the world should be registered. This was the first registration when Quirinius was governor of Syria. And all went to be registered, each to his own town. And Joseph also went up from Galilee, from the town of Nazareth, to Judea, to the city of

David, which is called Bethlehem, because he was of the house and lineage of David, to be registered with Mary, his betrothed, who was with child. And while they were there, the time came for her to give birth. And she gave birth to her firstborn son and wrapped him in swaddling cloths and laid him in a manger, because there was no place for them in the inn. (ESV)

Matthew 2: 1–6

Now after Jesus was born in Bethlehem of Judea in the days of Herod the king, behold, wise men from the east came to Jerusalem, saying, "Where is he who has been born king of the Jews? For we saw his star when it rose and have come to worship him." When Herod the king heard this, he was troubled, and all Jerusalem with him; and assembling all the chief priests and scribes of the people, he inquired of them where the Christ was to be born. They told him, "In Bethlehem of Judea, for so it is written by the prophet:

"'And you, O Bethlehem, in the land of Judah,
are by no means least among the rulers of Judah;
for from you shall come a ruler
who will shepherd my people Israel.'" (ESV)

Micah 5: 2

"But you, Bethlehem Ephrathah, though you are small among the clans of Judah, out of you will come for me one who will be ruler over Israel, whose origins are from of old, from ancient times." (NIV)

∽

Prayer focus:
I thank You again that You saw fit to become a man and

dwell among us! Because of Your humble beginnings, no one can say they are not welcome. I thank You for how You build up my faith each time I see how every prophecy written about You came to pass. Continue to surround me with Your presence during this season and throughout the year.

You may wish to sing a Christmas carol which focuses on Bethlehem such as 'O Little Town of Bethlehem' or 'What Child Is This?'

THE THIRD SUNDAY OF ADVENT

The third candle of Advent, lit on the third of four Sundays before Christmas, is sometimes known as the "Shepherds' Candle". It symbolizes "Joy" since as soon as the shepherds heard and saw for themselves, they spread the news far and wide about the Messiah's birth. It is amazing to ponder all that Christ did when He came to this earth. He demonstrated His humility and gives us an example to follow by appearing to lowly shepherds first. As well, shepherds are symbolic of the care and protection that Jesus has given to us as our Great Shepherd. Just like those shepherds from long ago, we should be filled with joy because of all that Jesus has done and should spread the good news wherever we can.

<u>Scripture:</u>
Luke 2: 8–9; 15–20
And in the same region there were shepherds out in the field, keeping watch over their flock by night. And an angel of

the Lord appeared to them, and the glory of the Lord shone around them, and they were filled with great fear...

When the angels went away from them into heaven, the shepherds said to one another, "Let us go over to Bethlehem and see this thing that has happened, which the Lord has made known to us." And they went with haste and found Mary and Joseph, and the baby lying in a manger. And when they saw it, they made known the saying that had been told them concerning this child. And all who heard it wondered at what the shepherds told them. But Mary treasured up all these things, pondering them in her heart. And the shepherds returned, glorifying and praising God for all they had heard and seen, as it had been told them. (ESV)

John 10: 11–15

"I am the Good Shepherd. The Good Shepherd lays down His life for the sheep. The hired hand is not the shepherd and does not own the sheep. So when he sees the wolf coming, he abandons the sheep and runs away. Then the wolf attacks the flock and scatters it. The man runs away because he is a hired hand and cares nothing for the sheep. I am the Good Shepherd; I know My sheep and my sheep know Me--just as the Father knows Me and I know the Father--and I lay down My life for the sheep. (NIV)

Romans 1: 16

For I am not ashamed of the gospel, for it is the power of God for salvation to everyone who believes, to the Jew first and also to the Greek. (NASB)

❀

<u>Prayer focus:</u>

Thank You, Jesus, that You are the Great Shepherd who will never abandon me or forsake me. Help me to follow Your example of humility and acceptance of others, no matter their walk of life. Also, empower me to follow the example of the shepherds who witnessed the angels' announcement. They immediately went and spread the good news. May I never be ashamed of the gospel, for it is the power of God for salvation to everyone who believes.

You may wish to sing a Christmas carol which focuses on the shepherds such as 'While Shepherds Watched Their Flocks By Night' or 'The First Noel'. Another fitting carol is 'Joy to the World' which speaks to the great joy we can all have because Jesus came as our Saviour.

THE FOURTH SUNDAY OF ADVENT

On the fourth Sunday in Advent, the "Angels' Candle" is lit, symbolizing "Peace". It is exciting to read about times when angelic beings and human beings came into contact with one another. There are many examples in the Bible, but it is worth remembering that angels are created beings the same as you or me. They have been given specific jobs to do. Ministers, messengers, warriors and guardians are just some of the roles they fulfill. In this account, we see that they were employed to deliver a message to Mary as well as to the shepherds. They also had the wonderful privilege of worshiping and praising God, heralding in His marvellous Son--something we can join them in doing on a daily basis.

Scripture:
Luke 2: 8–14
And in the same region there were shepherds out in the field, keeping watch over their flock by night. And an angel of

the Lord appeared to them, and the glory of the Lord shone around them, and they were filled with great fear. And the angel said to them, "Fear not, for behold, I bring you good news of great joy that will be for all the people. For unto you is born this day in the city of David a Savior, who is Christ the Lord. And this will be a sign for you: you will find a baby wrapped in swaddling cloths and lying in a manger." And suddenly there was with the angel a multitude of the heavenly host praising God and saying, "Glory to God in the highest, and on earth peace among those with whom He is pleased!" (ESV)

Luke 1: 26–38

In the sixth month the angel Gabriel was sent from God to a city of Galilee named Nazareth, to a virgin betrothed to a man whose name was Joseph, of the house of David. And the virgin's name was Mary. And he came to her and said, "Greetings, O favored one, the Lord is with you!" But she was greatly troubled at the saying, and tried to discern what sort of greeting this might be. And the angel said to her, "Do not be afraid, Mary, for you have found favor with God. And behold, you will conceive in your womb and bear a son, and you shall call his name Jesus. He will be great and will be called the Son of the Most High. And the Lord God will give to Him the throne of his father David, and He will reign over the house of Jacob forever, and of His kingdom there will be no end."

And Mary said to the angel, "How will this be, since I am a virgin?"

And the angel answered her, "The Holy Spirit will come upon you, and the power of the Most High will overshadow you; therefore the child to be borne will be called holy--the Son of God. And behold, your relative Elizabeth in her old age has also conceived a son, and this is the sixth month with her who was called barren. For nothing will be impossible with God." And Mary said, "Behold, I am the servant of the Lord; let it be to me according to your word." And the angel departed from her. (ESV)

Philippians 4: 7

And the peace of God, which surpasses all understanding, will guard your hearts and your minds in Christ Jesus. (ESV)

~

Prayer focus:

I join with the angels in praising you today, Oh Lord my God! You are worthy of all praise and glory and honour and majesty. You are exalted high above the earth! As I praise You today, may Your peace that surpasses understanding guard my heart and mind in Christ Jesus.

~

You may wish to sing a Christmas carol which focuses on the angels such as 'Angels We Have Heard on High' or 'Hark the Harold Angels Sing'.

CHRISTMAS EVE CELEBRATION OF ADVENT

The final day of the Advent celebration takes place on Christmas Eve. Many traditions include a fifth candle which is placed in the middle of the Advent wreath and which is lit at this time. It is known as "Christ's Candle". Celebrate by reflecting and remembering all that Christ has done!

<u>Scripture:</u>

Colossians 1: 15–23

The Son is the image of the invisible God, the firstborn over all creation. For in Him all things were created: things in heaven and on earth, visible and invisible, whether thrones or powers or rulers or authorities; all things have been created through Him and for Him. He is before all things, and in Him all things hold together. And He is the head of the body, the church; He is the beginning and the firstborn from among the dead, so that in everything He might have the supremacy. For

God was pleased to have all His fullness dwell in Him, and through Him to reconcile to Himself all things, whether things on earth or things in heaven, by making peace through His blood, shed on the cross.

Once you were alienated from God and were enemies in your minds because of your evil behavior. But now He has reconciled you by Christ's physical body through death to present you holy in His sight, without blemish and free from accusation--if you continue in your faith, established and firm, and do not move from the hope held out in the gospel. This is the gospel that you heard and that has been proclaimed to every creature under heaven, and of which I, Paul, have become a servant. (ESV)

Hebrews 1: 3

The Son is the radiance of God's glory and the exact representation of His being, sustaining all things by His powerful word. After He had provided purification for sins, He sat down at the right hand of the Majesty in heaven. (ESV)

∾

Prayer focus:

I exalt You, Jesus, for You are God incarnate—the exact representation of God, holy and unblemished; the creator of the universe, the beginning and the end, the supreme ruler of all... my redeemer and my friend. There are no words that can fully express my gratitude. I am unworthy and yet, through Your shed blood, You have deemed me worthy. I praise You today and pray that as the holiday season continues, I would be always mindful of You.

You may wish to sing a Christmas carol that focuses on Christ's birth such as 'Silent Night' or 'Away in a Manger'.

AFTERWORD

I hope you found this short booklet useful. It is by no means meant to be exhaustive, nor it is meant to replace any other traditions you may already be enjoying. It is simply a suggested way to incorporate Advent into the other traditions of the season. May you be blessed as you honour Jesus!

MORE IN THE SERIES

Simply Advent is an excerpt from a year long devotional series based on the Jewish calendar. All four seasons of *DIVINE APPOINTMENTS* are available in both paperback and hardcover. The set makes a wonderful gift.

If you enjoyed this booklet, please consider writing a review online. Reviews help readers find books they'll love and are tremendously helpful for today's authors. Thank you in advance!

Join Tracy's mailing list and get up to date info on all new releases, promos and giveaways when they happen. You'll also get a free book!

Visit Tracy's website for more titles including other devotional books, fiction and stage plays:
https://tracykrauss.com

ABOUT THE AUTHOR

Tracy Krauss is a multi-published novelist, playwright, and artist with several award winning and best selling novels, stage plays, devotionals and children's books in print. Her work strikes a chord with those looking for thought provoking faith based fiction laced with romance, suspense and humor. She holds a B.Ed from the University of Saskatchewan and has lived in many remote and interesting places in Canada's far north. She and her husband currently reside in beautiful Tumbler Ridge, BC where she continues to pursue all of her creative interests.

"Fiction on the edge – without crossing the line"
https://tracykrauss.com
or contact: tracy@tracykrauss.com